THE BEST OF LED-ZEPPELIN VOL. 1

PLAY DRUMS

Your Guarantee of Quality
As publishers, we strive to produce every book
to the highest commercial standards.
The music has been freshly engraved and the book has
been carefully designed to minimise awkward page turns
and to make playing from it a real pleasure.
Particular care has been given to specifying acid-free,
neutral-sized paper made from pulps which have not been
elemental chlorine bleached. This pulp is from farmed
sustainable forests and was produced with special regard
for the environment.
Throughout, the printing and binding have been planned
to ensure a sturdy, attractive publication which should
give years of enjoyment.
If your copy fails to meet our high standards,
please inform us and we will gladly replace it.

www.musicsales.com

THE BEST OF LED-ZEPPELIN

PLAY DRUMS WITH

VOL. 1

WISE PUBLICATIONS
PART OF THE MUSIC SALES GROUP

LONDON / NEW YORK / PARIS / SYDNEY / COPENHAGEN / BERLIN / MADRID / HONG KONG / TOKYO

Published by
Wise Publications
14-15 Berners Street, London W1T 3LJ, UK

Exclusive Distributors:
Music Sales Limited
Distribution Centre, Newmarket Road,
Bury St Edmunds, Suffolk IP33 3YB, UK

Music Sales Pty Limited
20 Resolution Drive,
Caringbah, NSW 2229, Australia

Order No. AM996633
ISBN 978-1-84772-949-1
This book © Copyright 2010 Wise Publications,
a division of Music Sales Limited.

Unauthorised reproduction of any part of this
publication by any means including photocopying
is an infringement of copyright.

Cover designed by Liz Barrand
Photo research by Jacqui Black

Printed in the EU

www.musicsales.com

COMMUNICATION BREAKDOWN 10

DAZED AND CONFUSED 14

WHOLE LOTTA LOVE 22

HEARTBREAKER 28

IMMIGRANT SONG 33

SINCE I'VE BEEN LOVING YOU 36

BLACK DOG 44

ROCK AND ROLL 50

NOTATION GUIDE 9

RECORDING NOTES

It is simply impossible to actually recreate the recorded performances of Led Zeppelin and the production techniques of Jimmy Page. The intention of these recordings is to aid study of John Bonham's drum parts by providing credible backing tracks to play-along with, hopefully capturing the spirit of the original music. The instruments and recording techniques used were chosen according to the information available about the original recording set-ups; however, with other less-controllable factors to consider (studio size, mic type and placement, location, tape machines and recording consoles, for example), choices about the right sound were driven as much by ear as the reported original conditions. Ultimately it is essential to listen to, and try and emulate the original Led Zeppelin tracks to really understand the musical nuance, intensity and brilliance of those recordings.

CREDITS

Supervisory editors: Brad Tolinski and Jimmy Brown

Project manager and music editor: Tom Farncombe

Additional transcription and editing: Jimmy Brown, Dan Begelman and Jack Allen

Audio recorded and mixed by Jonas Persson

Guitars and guitar transcriptions: Arthur Dick
Bass guitar and bass transcriptions: Paul Townsend
Drums, percussion and drum transcriptions: Noam Lederman

Keyboards and keyboard transcriptions: Paul Honey

Music engraved by Paul Ewers Music Design

With special thanks to Mark Lodge at Hiwatt UK for supplying the Hiwatt 100 Head – an exact replica of Jimmy Page's amp from the Led Zeppelin sessions.

WWW.HIWATT.CO.UK

Also thanks to Chandler guitars (www.chandlerguitars.co.uk).

Arthur Dick

Paul Townsend

Noam Lederman

EQUIPMENT LIST

DRUMS:
1968 Ludwig drum kit (24" bass drum; 13" rack tom; 16" floor tom; 18" second floor tom)
Paiste cymbals

Ludwig 6.5x14" Supraphonic snare drum; Ludwig 8x14" Coliseum snare drum

GUITARS:
1952 Goldtop Gibson Les Paul (reissue)
1959 Gibson Les Paul
1969 Fender Telecaster
1969 'Black Beauty' Gibson Les Paul
1972 Fender Telecaster

AMPLIFIERS:
Cornell Romany 10-watt combo
Hiwatt 100
Marshall JCM2000
1965 VOX AC30
1964 Watkins Electronics Westminster 5-watt combo

GUITAR EFFECTS:
Celmo Sardine Can Compressor
Pete Cornish Sustain Pedal
Jim Dunlop Crybaby Wah-Wah
Eventide Flanger
Fulltone Full-Drive 2
Lexicon PCM91
Line 6 MM4 Modulation Pedal
Manley Valve EQ
Roger Mayer Treble Booster
Roger Mayer Voodoo Vibe+ Vibrato Unit
Tubetech CL1B Valve Compressor
Universal Audio DI
Violin Bow

BASS GUITARS:
1991 'Longhorn' Fender Jazz bass
1978 Fender Precision bass
1962 Fender Jazz bass (reissue)
(strung with flatwound strings, used to emulate the organ pedal performance on 'Since I've Been Loving You')

Ashdown bass amplification

Nord Electro2 modelling keyboard

Studer A80 tape machine

1968 Ludwig drum kit

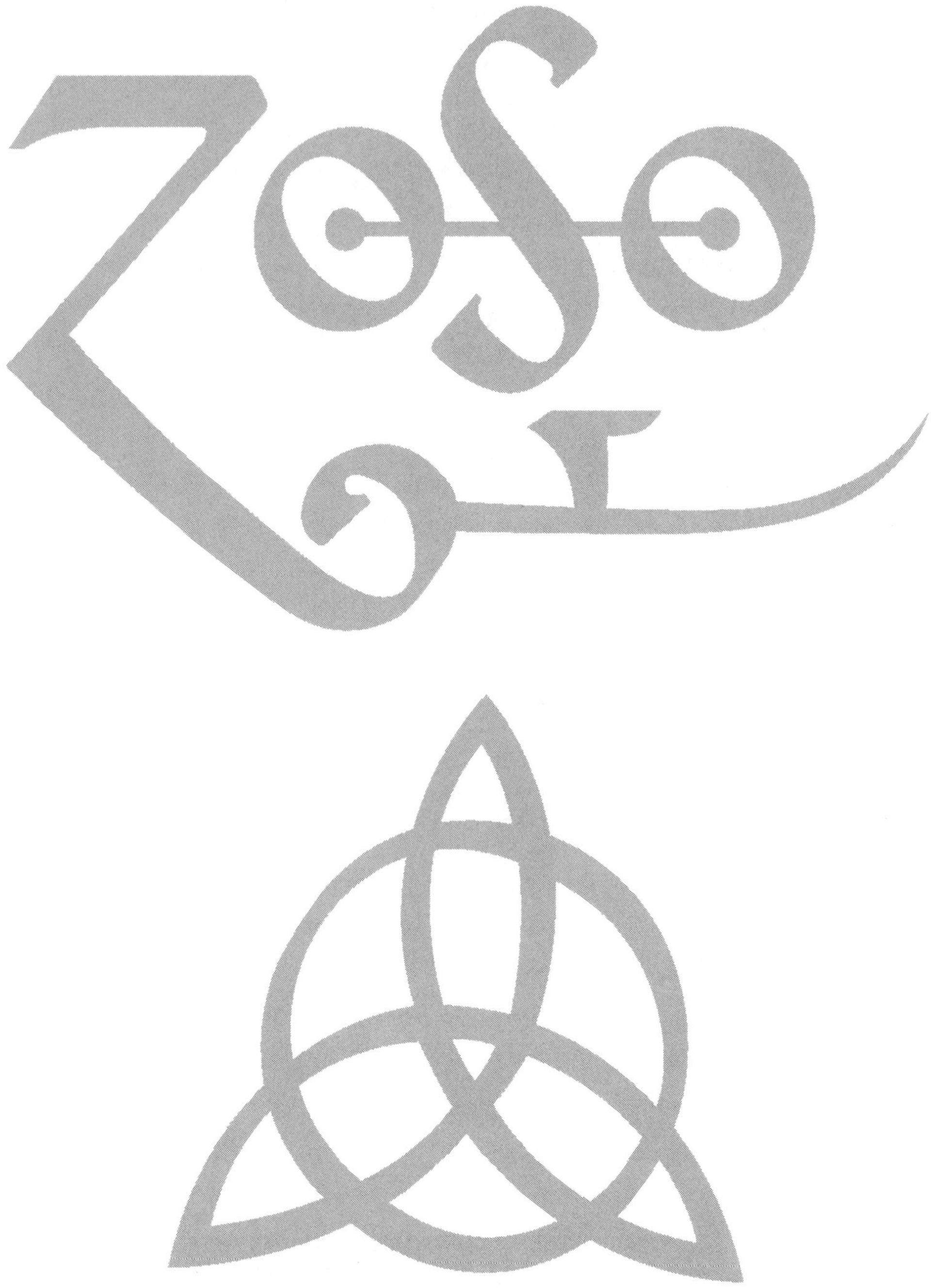

NOTATION GUIDE

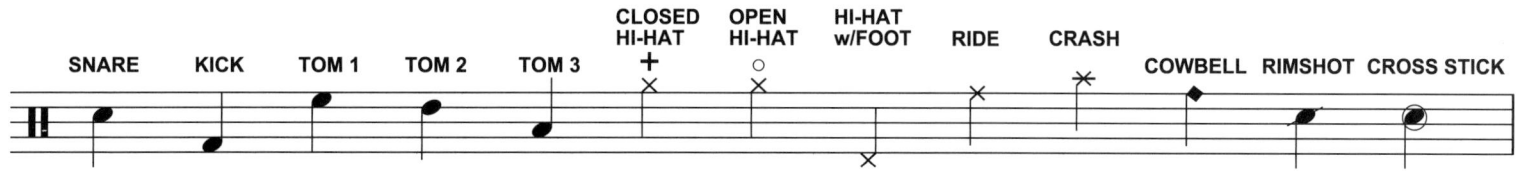

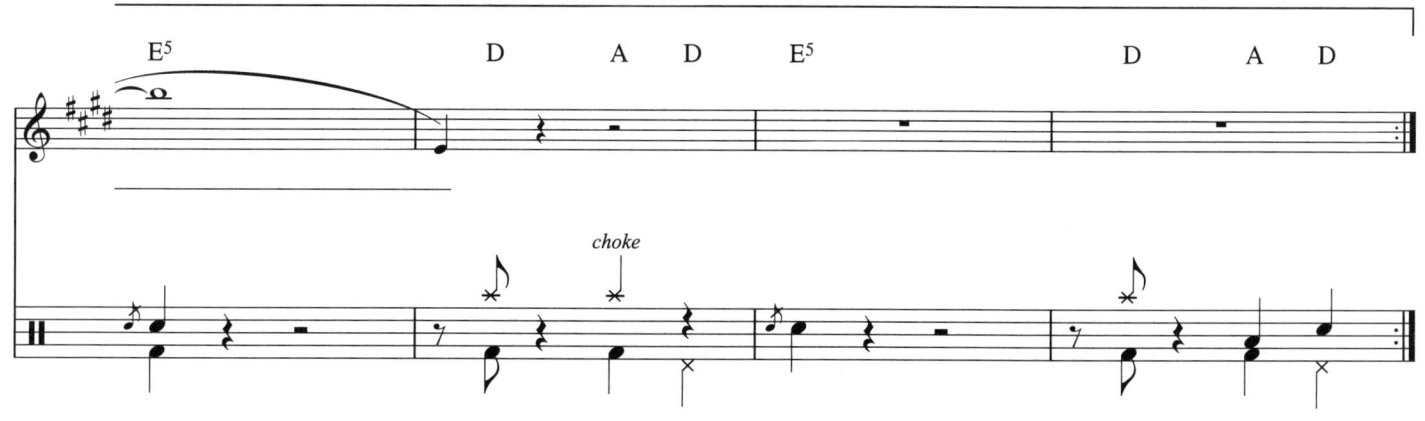

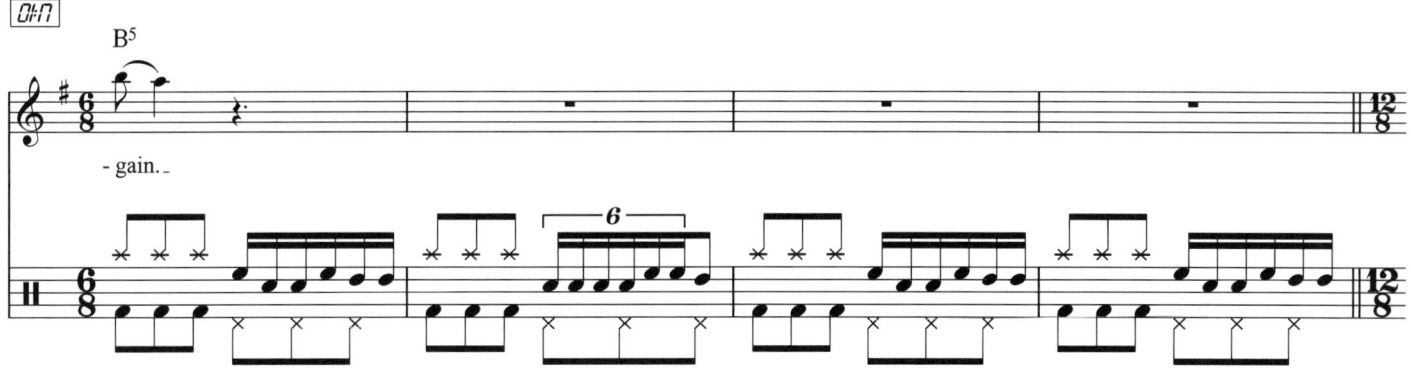

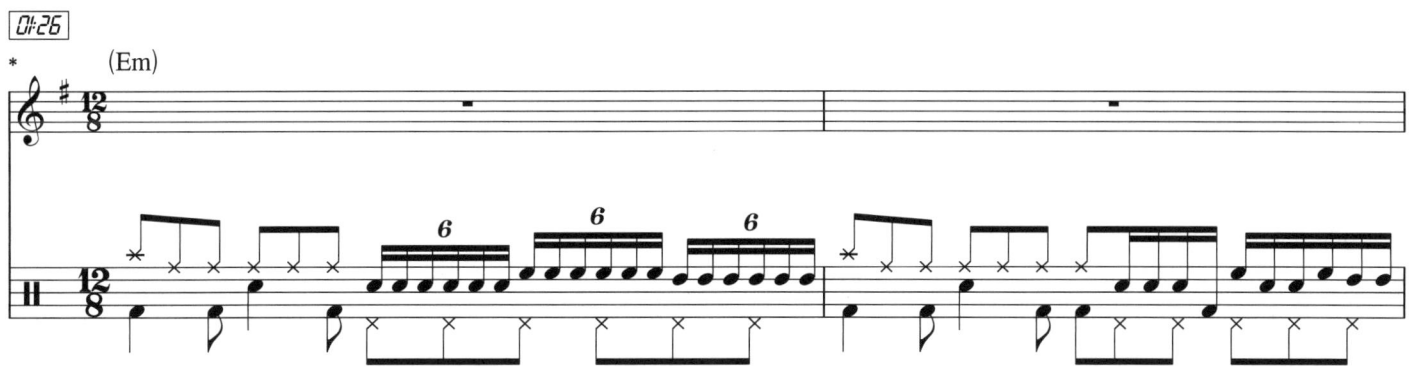

* *The original versions of this song by Jake Holmes, and by Jimmy Page with the Yardbirds, clearly place the low E of the signature bass line riff on beat 1 and the high G on beat 2. In the first 2 verses John Bonham chooses to turn the metre around, placing the high G on beat 1. From this point on he clearly turns the metre around again, placing the high G on beat 2 as in the original versions. He remains in this metre for the rest of the song. All subsequent versions of this song follow this exact same pattern of turning the metre around.*

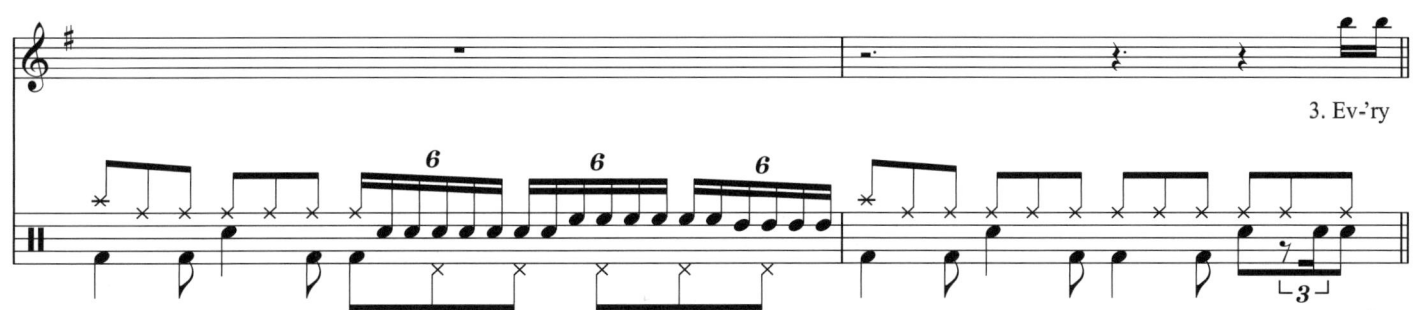

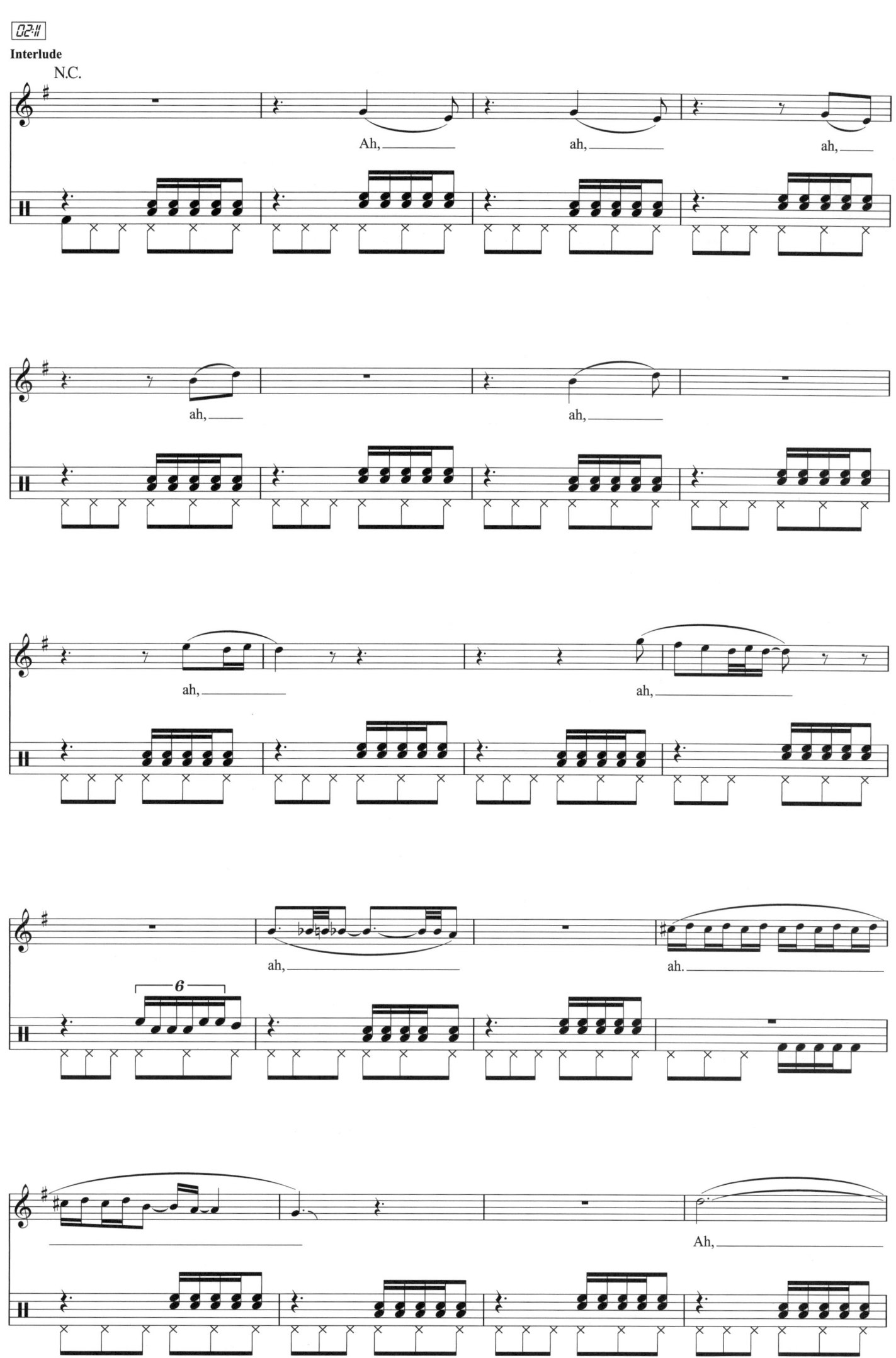

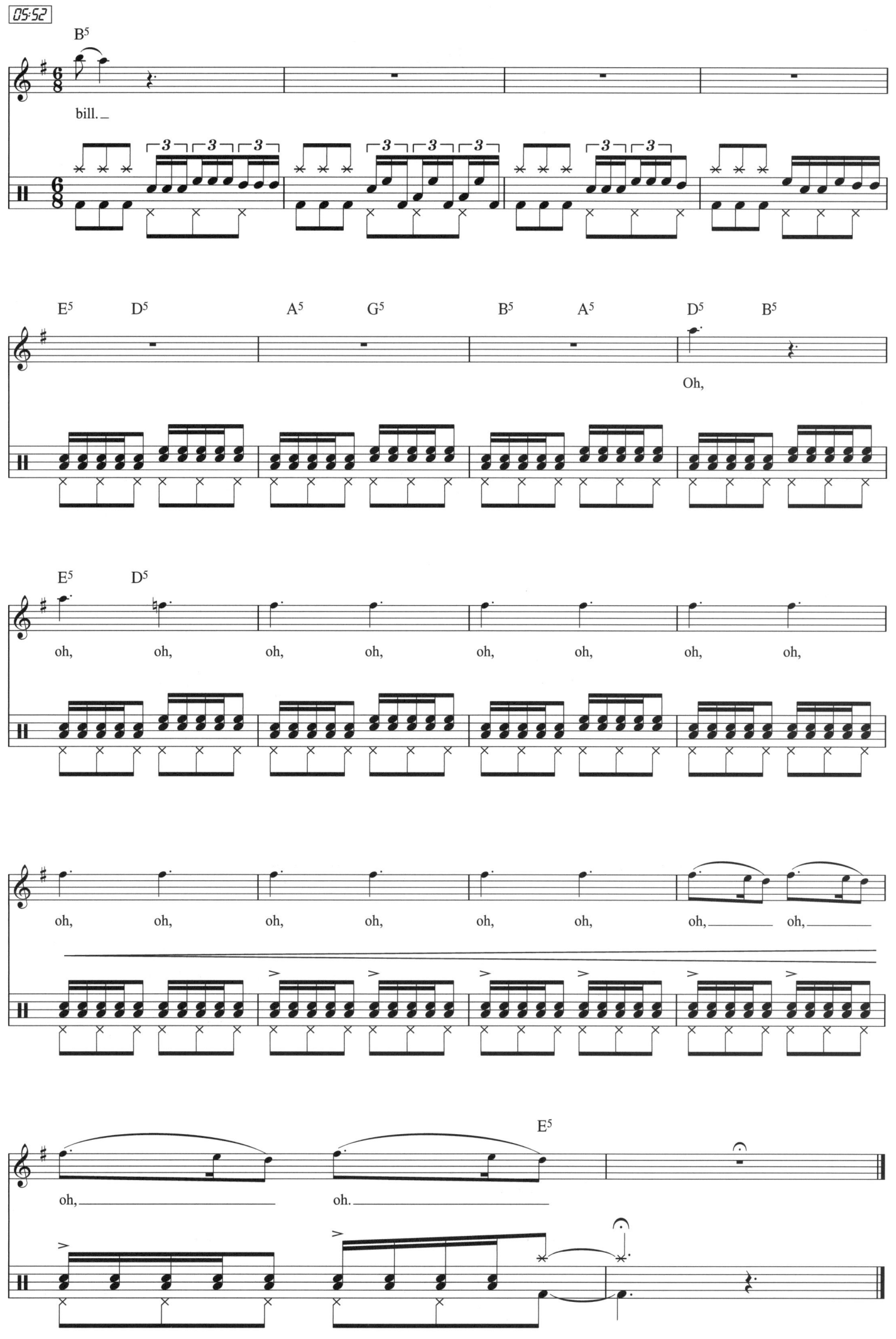

WHOLE LOTTA LOVE

*Words & Music by
Jimmy Page, Robert Plant, John Paul Jones & John Bonham*

© Copyright 1969 Succubus Music Limited/Sons Of Einion Limited/Cap Three Limited/Estate of J. Bonham.
Print Rights Administered by Music Sales Limited.
All Rights Reserved. International Copyright Secured.

Full performance demo: CD 1, track 3
Backing only: CD 2, track 3

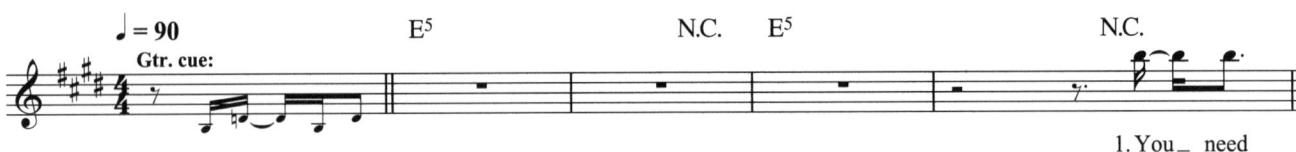

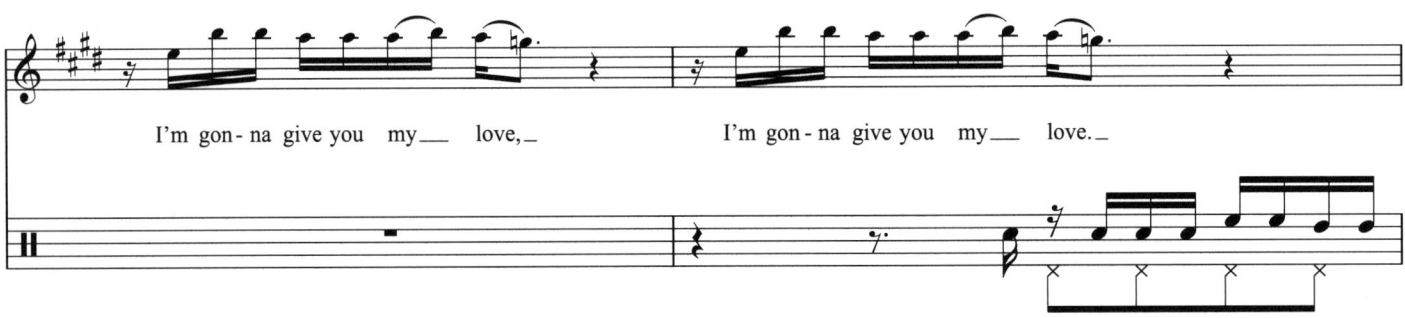

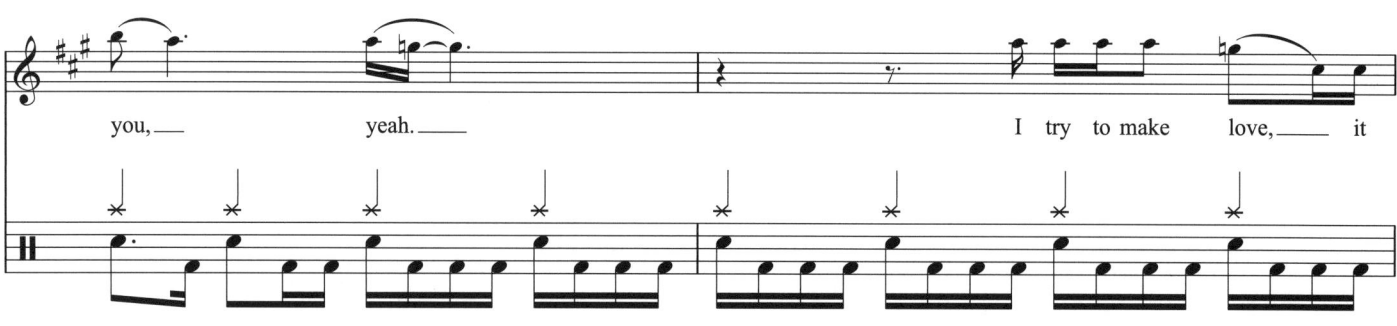
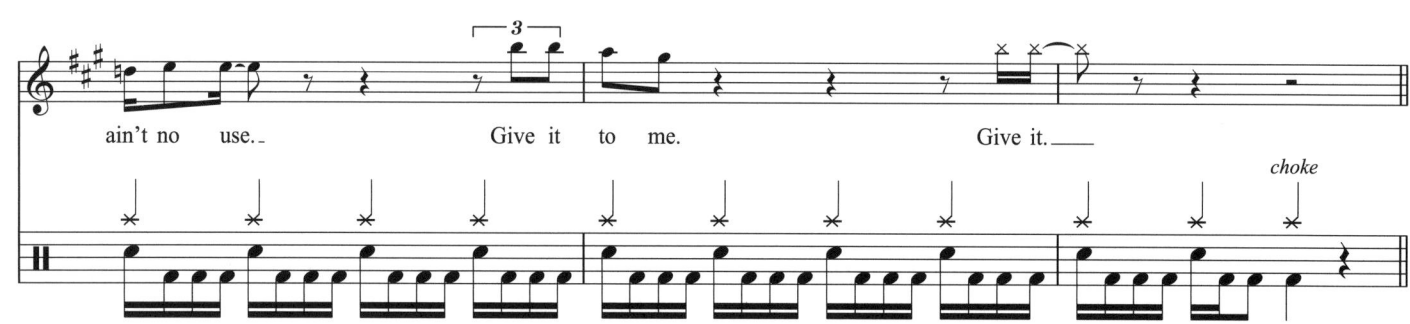

Since I've Been Loving You

Words & Music by
Jimmy Page, Robert Plant & John Paul Jones

© Copyright 1970 Succubus Music Limited/Sons Of Einion Limited/Cap Three Limited.
Print Rights Administered by Music Sales Limited.
All Rights Reserved. International Copyright Secured.

Full performance demo: CD 1, track 6
Backing only: CD 2, track 6

Verse

1. Working from seven to eleven ev'ry night, (it) really makes (my) life a drag, I don't think that's right.

I've really been the best, the best of fools, I did what I could, yeah.

because I love you baby, how I love you darling, how I love you baby, mama love, lil' girl, little girl.

But baby, since I've been loving you, yeah,

I'm about to lose my worried mind, oh, yeah.

Slightly swung

02:29

Verse
2. Ev-'rybody trying to tell me, that you didn't mean me no good.

I've been trying, Lord, let me tell, let me tell you I really did the best I could.

Fm
I've been, I've been work - ing from se - ven
ah, to e - lev - en ev' ___ ry night, I said it kind - a makes your life a drag, drag, drag, drag, Lord, ___
E♭6
E♭6 G/D E♭6 G/D E♭6 G/D E♭6 G/D E♭6 G/D E♭6 G/D E♭6 G/D E♭6 G/D E♭6 G/D E♭6 G/D E♭6 G/D E♭6
yeah, ___ that ain't right, _ now, now.
G5
Since ___ I've been lov - ing you, ___
A♭
Fm
I'm a - bout to lose _ my wor - ried
Cm/E♭ G7/D Cm E♭
D7
D♭maj7
mind. _
Slightly swung

03:39 Guitar solo

Cm | Fm
Cm
Fm
Cm
Gm | A♭ | Fm
Cm/E♭ G⁷/D Cm | D⁷ | D♭maj⁷ *Slightly swung*

04:50 Interlude

Cm

Said I've been cry - ing,___ yeah.   Oh, my tears they fell like rain.___

E♭

Don't you hear___ them,   don't you hear them fall-ing?

Verse `05:31`

Don't you hear them, don't you hear them fall - ing?

3. Do you re-mem-ber, Ma-ma, when I knocked up-on your door? I said you had the nerve to tell me you did-n't want me no more, yeah.

(I) Open my front door, I hear my back door slam, you know I must have one of them new-fan-gled, new-fan-gled back-door man,___ yeah, yeah, yeah, yeah yeah.

I've been__ work-ing__ from se - ven, se - ven, se-ven to e-

-le - ven ev - 'ry night, it kind - a makes my life a drag,__

a drag,__ drag. Ah_____ yeah, it makes (it) a drag.

Ba - by since I've been lov - ing you,__

Lyrics:

I'm a-bout to lose, I'm a-bout to lose, lose my wor-ried mind.

And just one more, just one more...

Slightly swung

Oh, yeah.

Since I've been lov-ing you, I'm gon-na lose my wor-ried mind.

rall. **Freely**

Black Dog

**Words & Music by
Jimmy Page, Robert Plant & John Paul Jones**

© Copyright 1972 Succubus Music Limited/Sons Of Einion Limited/Cap Three Limited.
Print Rights Administered by Music Sales Limited.
All Rights Reserved. International Copyright Secured.

Full performance demo: CD 1, track 7
Backing only: CD 2, track 7

1. Hey, hey, ma - ma, said the way you move, gon-na make you sweat, gon-na make you groove.

2. Ah, ah, child, way you shake that thing, gon-na make you burn, gon-na make you sting.
3. Hey, hey, ba - by, when you walk that way, watch (your) ho-ney drip, can't keep a - way.

E5
A5
Oh
bell of ride
00:49
yeah, oh yeah, oh, oh, oh. Oh
yeah, oh, yeah, oh, oh, oh. 4.Well
Freely
A5
I got to roll, can't stand still, got a flam-ing heart, can't get my fill.
5. Eyes that shine, burn-ing red, dreams of you all through my head.
(sticks)

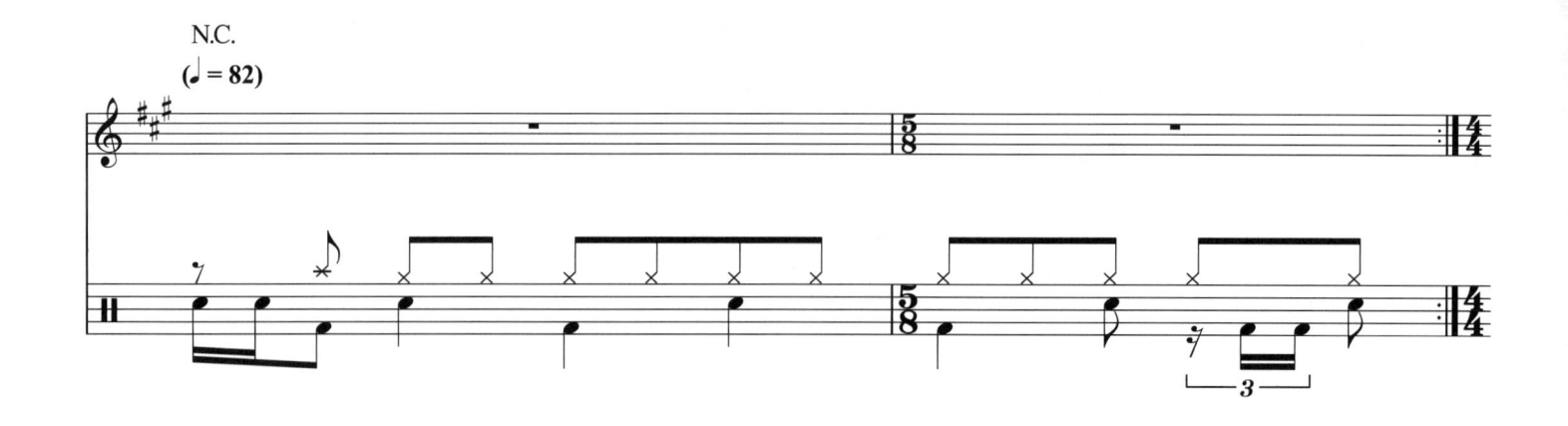

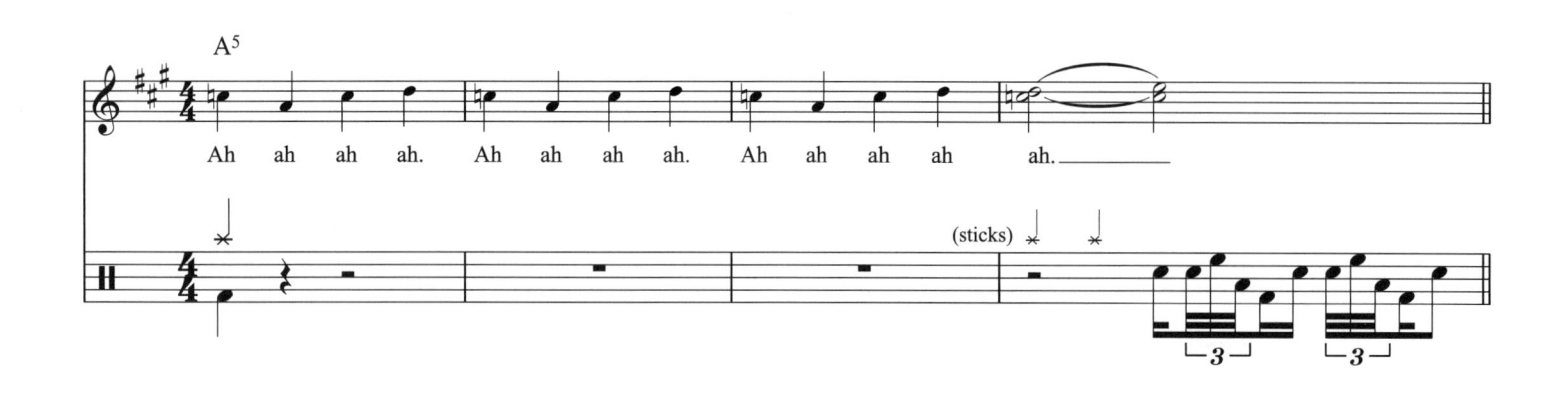

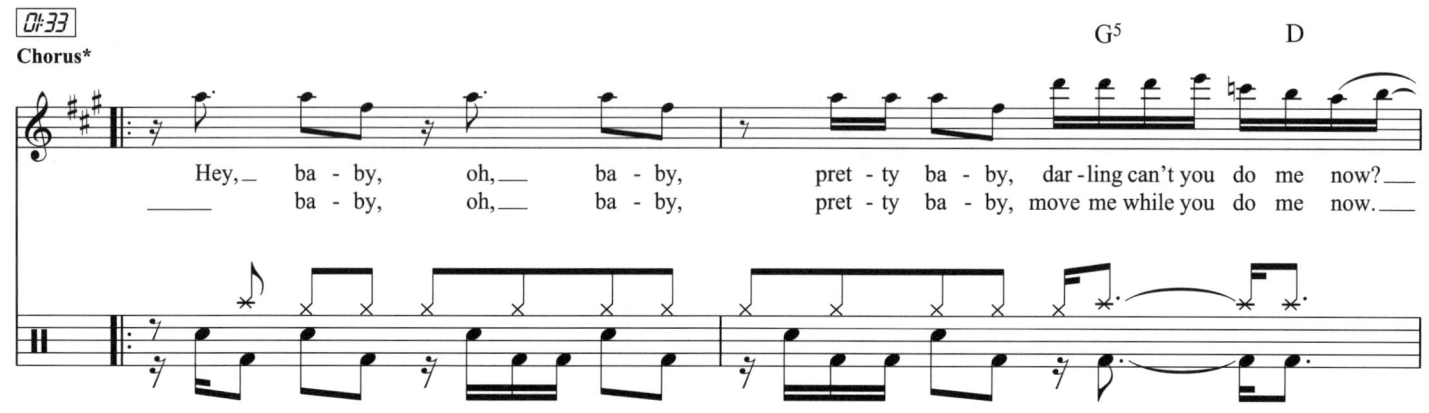

*The metre of this song is somewhat controversial, especially in the **Chorus** and **Solo** sections.
Previous editions suggest that the kick drum indicates the downbeat, meaning irregular bars at certain points.
However, the drum clicks and cues before these sections would make it seem that the metre actually remains constant, in 4/4;
therefore the snare drum remains on the backbeat throughout. This is reflected in this arrangement.

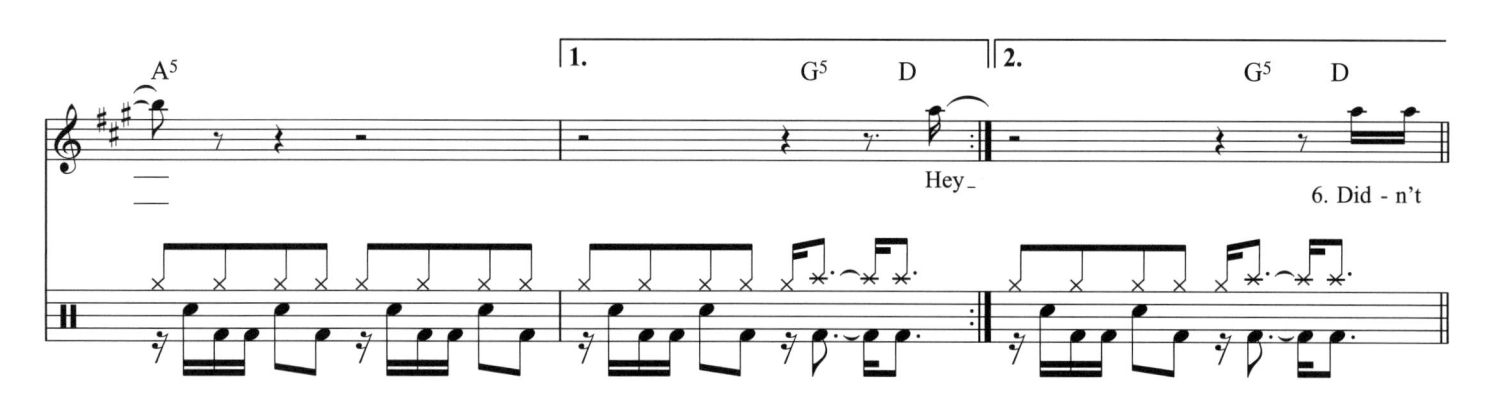

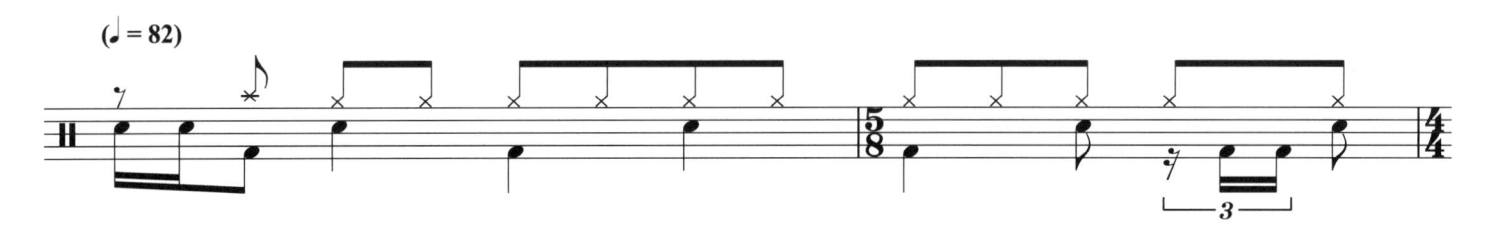

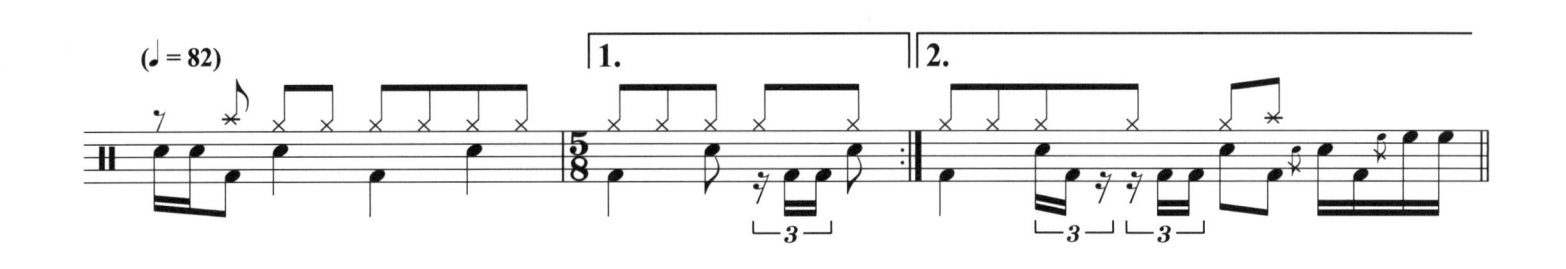

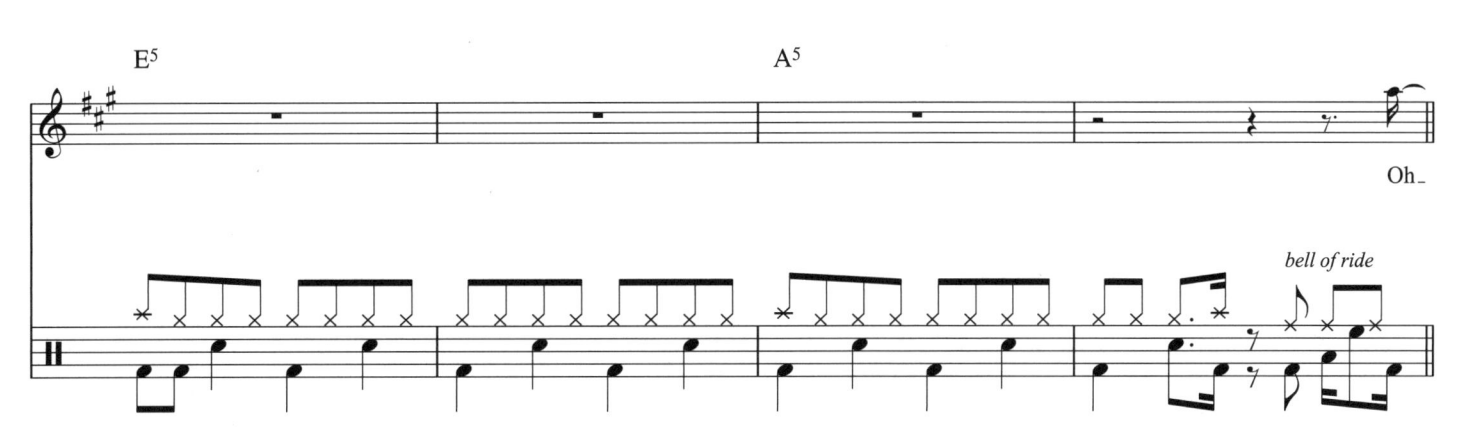

01:56 Freely

Verse

take too long 'fore I found out what peo-ple mean by 'down and out.'

(♩ = 82)

02:07 Freely

Verse

7. Spent my mon-ey, took my car, start-ed tell-ing her friends she gon-na be a star.
8. I don't know, but I've been told, a big-legged woman ain't got no soul.

(♩ = 82)

Oh

bell of ride

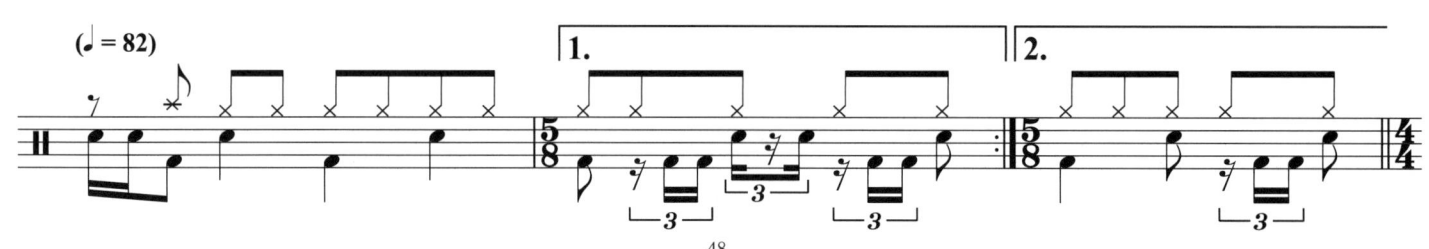

02:39

— yeah, oh yeah, oh, oh, oh. Oh

— yeah, oh, yeah, oh, oh, oh.

02:50

Verse **Freely**
(A⁵)

9. All I ask for, all I pray, stead-y-rolling wo-man gon-na come my way.
10. Need a woman gonna hold my hand, won't tell me no lies, make me a hap-py man.

(sticks)

(♩ = 82)   1.   2.

48

Ah ah, ah ah, ah ah, ah ah, ah ah, ah ah,

03:23
Outro Solo

Repeat ad lib. to fade

Rock and Roll

Words & Music by
Jimmy Page, Robert Plant, John Paul Jones & John Bonham

© Copyright 1972 Succubus Music Limited/Sons Of Einion Limited/Cap Three Limited/Estate of J. Bonham.
Print Rights Administered by Music Sales Limited.
All Rights Reserved. International Copyright Secured.

Full performance demo: CD 1, track 8
Backing only: CD 2, track 8

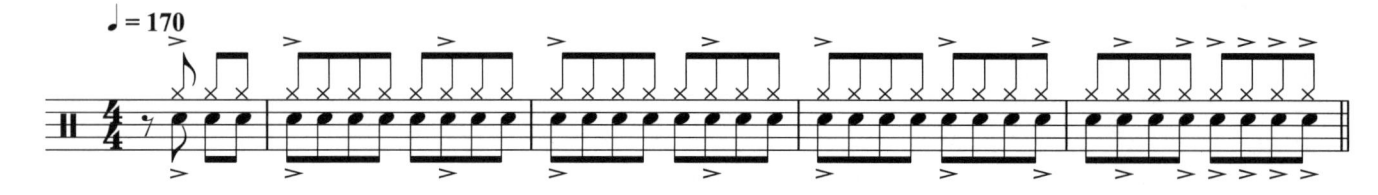

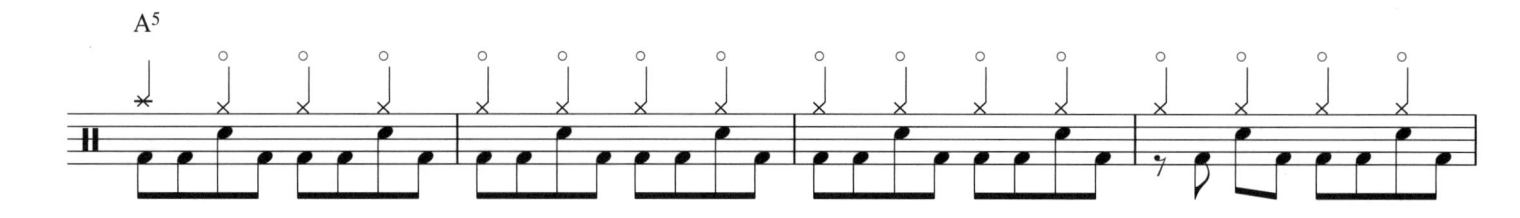

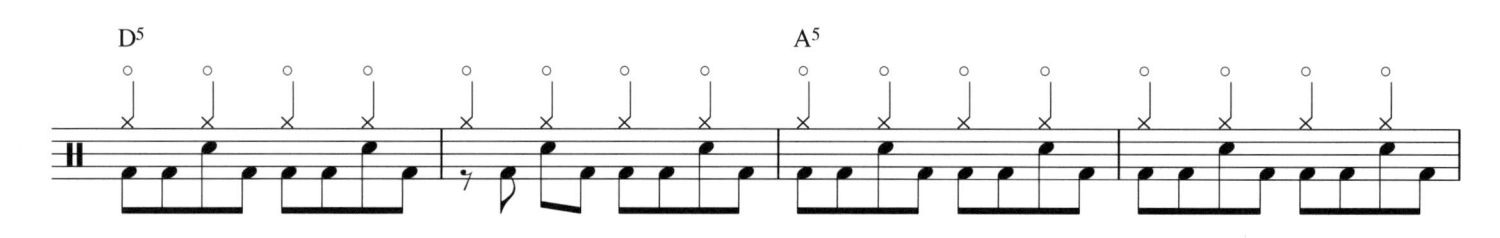

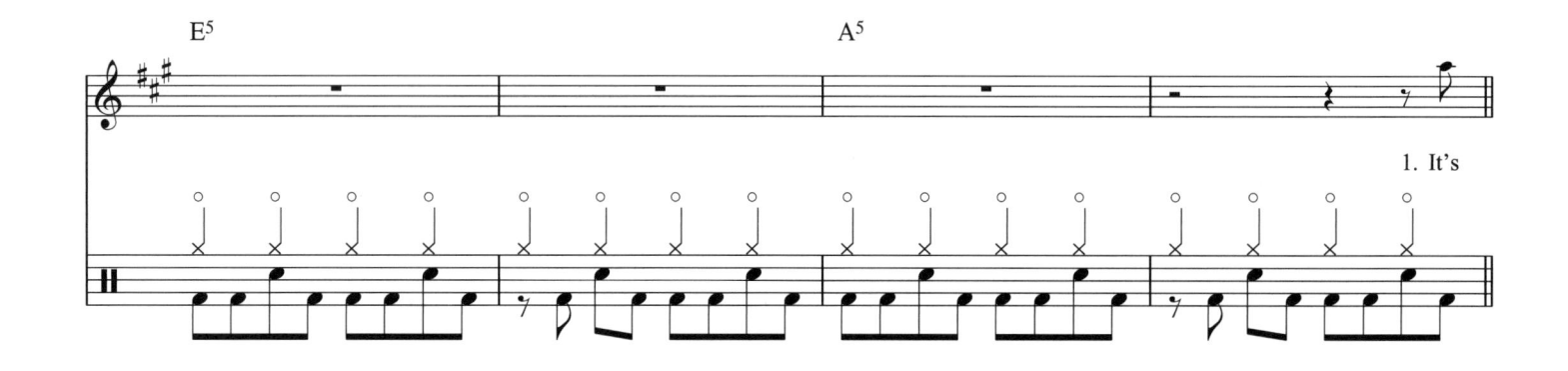

Intro
2 bar count in:
♩ = 170

been a long time since I did the stroll.
can't count the tears of a life with no love.
Ooh,
2º
(D5)
let me get it back, let me get (it) back, let me get back,
Car-ry me back, car-ry me back, car-ry me back,
ba-by, where I come from.
ba-by, where I come from.
2º
*crash 1º only
(A5)
Oh, oh.
It's
*crash 1º only
1.
(E5)
(D5)
been a long time, been a long time, been a long, lone-ly, lone-ly, lone-ly, lone-ly, lone-ly

A5
time. Yes, it has. 2. It's
2.
E5
D5
been a long time, been a long time, been a long, lone - ly, lone - ly, lone - ly, lone - ly, lone - ly
A5
time. Oh.
01:34
A5
D5
A5
E5
A5

seems so long since we walked in the moon-light.

Mak-ing vows, that just can't work right. Ha, ha, yeah.

3. Oh, it

D5
O - pen your arms, o - pen your arms, o - pen your arms. Ba - by let my love come
A5
runn - ing in. Yes. It's
E5
been a long time, been a long time, been a long,
D5
lone - ly, lone - ly, lone - ly, lone - ly, lone - ly
02:52
A5
time.
Outro
Yeah, hey. Yeah, hey.

Yeah, hey. Yeah, hey.

D5

A5
Ooh yeah, ooh yeah. Ooh yeah, ooh yeah. It's

E5 — D5 N.C. *Free time*
been a long time, been a long time, been a long, lone-ly, lone-ly, lone-

-ly, lone-ly, lone-ly time.

Drum fill

A5

choke

FULL INSTRUMENTAL PERFORMANCES (WITH DRUMS):

Load Disc 1 into your computer to access a PDF of easy-to-read drum charts for all 8 songs.

DISC 1:

1. Communication Breakdown

(Page/Plant/Jones/Bonham) Warner/Chappell North America Limited.

2. Dazed And Confused

(Page) Warner/Chappell North America Limited.

3. Whole Lotta Love

(Page/Plant/Jones/Bonham) Warner/Chappell North America Limited.

4. Heartbreaker

(Page/Plant/Jones/Bonham) Warner/Chappell North America Limited.

5. Immigrant Song

(Page/Plant) Warner/Chappell North America Limited.

6. Since I've Been Loving You

(Page/Plant/Jones) Warner/Chappell North America Limited.

7. Black Dog

(Page/Plant/Jones) Warner/Chappell North America Limited.

8. Rock And Roll

(Page/Plant/Jones/Bonham) Warner/Chappell North America Limited.

BACKING TRACKS ONLY (WITHOUT DRUMS):

DISC 2:
1. Communication Breakdown
2. Dazed And Confused
3. Whole Lotta Love
4. Heartbreaker
5. Immigrant Song
6. Since I've Been Loving You
7. Black Dog
8. Rock And Roll